PRINCEWILL LAGANG

The Power of Vulnerability in Relationships

First published by PRINCEWILL LAGANG 2023

Copyright © 2023 by Princewill Lagang

All rights reserved. No part of this publication may be reproduced, stored or transmitted in any form or by any means, electronic, mechanical, photocopying, recording, scanning, or otherwise without written permission from the publisher. It is illegal to copy this book, post it to a website, or distribute it by any other means without permission.

Princewill Lagang asserts the moral right to be identified as the author of this work.

First edition

This book was professionally typeset on Reedsy.
Find out more at reedsy.com

Contents

1	Introduction	1
2	Defining Vulnerability	4
3	Unmasking Fear and Shame	7
4	Building Trust Through Vulnerability	10
5	Authentic Communication	13
6	The Gift of Listening	16
7	Vulnerability and Emotional Intimacy	19
8	Embracing Imperfections Together	22
9	Conflict and Vulnerability	25
10	Strengthening Bonds Through Shared Vulnerability	28
11	Healing and Forgiveness	31
12	Sustaining a Vulnerable Connection	34

1

Introduction

In this opening chapter, we will delve into the fundamental concept of vulnerability and its profound impact on relationships. Vulnerability, often misconstrued as a sign of weakness, is actually a cornerstone of authentic and meaningful connections. By introducing readers to this central theme, we set the stage for exploring the intricacies of human interactions throughout the book.

Section 1: Understanding Vulnerability

We begin by defining vulnerability and dispelling misconceptions surrounding it. Vulnerability is portrayed not as a flaw, but as an essential aspect of being human. We discuss its psychological and emotional dimensions, highlighting the interplay between fear, courage, and authenticity. Drawing from psychology, sociology, and personal experiences, we lay the groundwork for readers to comprehend vulnerability's various facets.

Section 2: Vulnerability in Relationships

In this section, we explore how vulnerability shapes relationships. We delve into the dynamics of vulnerability in different relationship types—intimate partnerships, friendships, familial connections, and professional collaborations. Real-life examples and case studies illustrate how moments of vulnerability foster trust, empathy, and mutual understanding among individuals. We also address the challenges and potential pitfalls of being vulnerable, such as the fear of rejection or exploitation.

Section 3: The Power of Authentic Connections

Here, we discuss the profound impact of vulnerability on the authenticity of relationships. Authentic connections are forged when individuals dare to reveal their true selves, insecurities, and aspirations. We explore how such connections lead to deeper emotional bonds, greater intimacy, and richer personal growth. The concept of shared vulnerability, where both parties engage in open and honest communication, is presented as a catalyst for transformative relationships.

Section 4: Significance of the Book's Theme

In this section, we underscore the importance of the overarching theme of vulnerability for readers. In an increasingly disconnected and digitized world, where superficial interactions abound, embracing vulnerability becomes a remedy for loneliness and disconnection. We emphasize that this book is not just about understanding vulnerability, but also about cultivating it intentionally to enhance the quality of our relationships and our lives.

Section 5: Roadmap of the Book

The chapter concludes with an overview of the book's structure and what readers can expect in the coming chapters. We provide a glimpse into the topics that will be covered, such as vulnerability in conflict resolution, vulnerability in leadership, and strategies for nurturing vulnerability while

INTRODUCTION

maintaining healthy boundaries.

By the end of Chapter 1, readers will have a comprehensive understanding of vulnerability's role in relationships, and they will be primed to explore the depths of this theme in the subsequent chapters of the book.

2

Defining Vulnerability

In this chapter, we delve deeper into the concept of vulnerability, clarifying its meaning within the context of relationships and examining the nuanced ways in which it can vary from person to person.

Section 1: Revisiting Vulnerability

We begin by revisiting the definition of vulnerability established in the previous chapter, emphasizing its role as a catalyst for authentic connections. We touch upon vulnerability's inherent paradox—how it involves both the exposure of our emotional core and the potential for immense strength.

Section 2: Layers of Vulnerability

Here, we explore the multifaceted nature of vulnerability by dissecting its layers. We discuss emotional vulnerability, where individuals share their feelings and experiences, and cognitive vulnerability, which involves exposing one's thoughts, beliefs, and uncertainties. By highlighting these distinct layers, we show that vulnerability extends beyond mere emotional disclosure.

Section 3: Individual Differences in Vulnerability

This section delves into the understanding that vulnerability is not a one-size-fits-all concept. We explore how individuals have different comfort levels and thresholds for being vulnerable. Factors such as personality traits, past experiences, and cultural backgrounds can significantly influence how one perceives and engages with vulnerability. By recognizing these differences, we encourage readers to approach vulnerability with empathy and respect for others' boundaries.

Section 4: Vulnerability Spectrum

In this part, we introduce the idea of a vulnerability spectrum. We discuss how vulnerability can manifest in varying degrees, ranging from sharing minor concerns to disclosing deeply personal traumas. By illustrating this spectrum, we help readers visualize the vast range of vulnerability experiences that exist. This section emphasizes that vulnerability isn't an all-or-nothing concept; it's a fluid experience that can evolve over time.

Section 5: The Intersection of Vulnerability and Trust

Here, we explore the interplay between vulnerability and trust. We discuss how the willingness to be vulnerable can serve as a litmus test for the level of trust in a relationship. At the same time, vulnerability can also contribute to the cultivation of trust, as it signifies a commitment to authenticity and mutual understanding.

Section 6: Challenges and Rewards of Vulnerability

The chapter concludes by addressing both the challenges and rewards of embracing vulnerability. We discuss common barriers to being vulnerable, such as fear of judgment or rejection, and provide strategies to overcome them. Additionally, we highlight the transformative rewards of vulnerability, including enhanced intimacy, personal growth, and strengthened connections.

By the end of Chapter 2, readers will have a comprehensive understanding of vulnerability's complexity and variability. They'll be equipped with the tools to navigate the intricacies of vulnerability in different relationships, while respecting individual differences and cultivating authentic connections.

3

Unmasking Fear and Shame

In this chapter, we delve into the powerful emotions of fear and shame, exploring how they often act as significant barriers to vulnerability. We'll provide insights into their role, their impact on relationships, and strategies for overcoming them.

Section 1: Fear as a Barrier to Vulnerability

We begin by dissecting the different forms of fear that inhibit vulnerability. Fear of rejection, judgment, and emotional pain are common factors that prevent individuals from opening up. We discuss how these fears are often rooted in past experiences and societal norms, and how they hinder the development of meaningful connections.

Section 2: The Role of Shame

Here, we delve into the complex emotion of shame and its role in stifling vulnerability. We examine how shame can arise from a sense of unworthiness or inadequacy, leading individuals to believe that their vulnerabilities are unacceptable. By addressing shame head-on, we aim to help readers understand its origins and impact, while emphasizing that vulnerability is a courageous act rather than a source of shame.

Section 3: Fear, Shame, and Relationship Dynamics

This section explores how fear and shame can shape relationship dynamics. We discuss the paradoxical cycle wherein withholding vulnerability due to fear or shame can actually contribute to disconnection and strained relationships. Through relatable examples, we illustrate how the absence of vulnerability prevents authentic engagement and inhibits emotional intimacy.

Section 4: Recognizing Fear and Shame

In this part, we provide readers with tools to recognize fear and shame when they arise. We discuss the physical and emotional manifestations of these emotions and their impact on thoughts and behaviors. By cultivating self-awareness, individuals can better understand the root causes of their reluctance to be vulnerable.

Section 5: Strategies for Addressing Fear and Shame

The chapter concludes by offering practical strategies to address fear and shame as barriers to vulnerability. We explore techniques such as reframing negative beliefs, practicing self-compassion, and seeking support from trusted individuals. By actively addressing these emotions, individuals can gradually dismantle the walls preventing them from embracing vulnerability.

Section 6: Embracing Courage and Resilience

In the final section of the chapter, we emphasize the importance of courage and resilience in overcoming fear and shame. We share stories of individuals who have navigated their vulnerabilities despite these barriers, highlighting their journeys as sources of inspiration and empowerment.

By the end of Chapter 3, readers will have gained a comprehensive understanding of how fear and shame can hinder vulnerability and damage relationships. They'll be equipped with practical tools and insights to confront and navigate these emotions, empowering them to embark on a journey of authentic connections in the chapters to come.

4

Building Trust Through Vulnerability

In this chapter, we explore the symbiotic relationship between vulnerability and trust, highlighting how vulnerability serves as a foundational element for building and deepening trust within relationships. Through real-life stories and relatable examples, we'll demonstrate the transformative power of vulnerability in fostering trust.

Section 1: The Nexus of Vulnerability and Trust

We begin by establishing the essential link between vulnerability and trust. We discuss how vulnerability creates an environment of openness and authenticity, where individuals feel safe to share their true selves. This lays the groundwork for building trust, as it demonstrates a willingness to be seen and accepted, warts and all.

Section 2: Vulnerability as a Trust-Builder

Here, we delve into how vulnerability actively contributes to building trust.

We explore how sharing vulnerabilities can lead to reciprocity, encouraging the other party to also reveal their inner thoughts and feelings. We discuss the concept of the "vulnerability loop," where each instance of shared vulnerability strengthens the bond of trust, creating a positive feedback cycle.

Section 3: Real-Life Stories of Vulnerability and Trust

This section is dedicated to sharing real-life stories and examples that showcase the impact of vulnerability on trust. We narrate accounts of individuals who, through their openness, managed to bridge gaps, mend relationships, and forge unbreakable connections. These stories serve as powerful reminders that vulnerability is often the key to unlocking the depths of trust.

Section 4: Vulnerability in Action

In this part, we provide practical scenarios where vulnerability can be effectively employed to build trust. Whether it's admitting mistakes, expressing insecurities, or sharing aspirations, we discuss how vulnerability can be strategically woven into various aspects of relationships to create bonds of trust that endure challenges.

Section 5: The Ripple Effect of Vulnerability

Here, we explore how vulnerability's impact extends beyond individual relationships. We discuss how cultivating vulnerability within one relationship can spill over into other areas of life, enhancing overall emotional intelligence and communication skills. This section emphasizes vulnerability's role in creating a more empathetic and connected society.

Section 6: Navigating Vulnerability in Different Relationships

The chapter concludes by offering insights into how vulnerability plays out in different relationship dynamics—intimate partnerships, friendships, family relationships, and professional collaborations. We highlight the unique ways vulnerability contributes to building trust in each context and provide guidance on navigating the challenges that may arise.

By the end of Chapter 4, readers will have a comprehensive understanding of how vulnerability acts as a cornerstone for trust-building in relationships. Through relatable stories and practical examples, they'll be inspired to embrace vulnerability as a powerful tool for fostering connections based on authenticity and trust.

5

Authentic Communication

In this chapter, we delve into the profound impact of vulnerability on communication authenticity. We explore how embracing vulnerability can lead to more open and honest conversations, and we offer readers practical tips for cultivating authenticity in their interactions.

Section 1: The Connection Between Vulnerability and Authentic Communication

We start by discussing the intrinsic link between vulnerability and authentic communication. Vulnerability's role in revealing one's genuine thoughts, feelings, and intentions creates a fertile ground for meaningful conversations. By allowing ourselves to be vulnerable, we pave the way for authentic interactions that foster understanding and connection.

Section 2: Vulnerability as a Gateway to Openness

Here, we delve into how vulnerability serves as a gateway to opening up in communication. By sharing vulnerabilities, individuals signal their willingness to engage in genuine dialogue, inviting others to reciprocate. We discuss how this exchange of vulnerability leads to deeper, more meaningful conversations that transcend surface-level interactions.

Section 3: Practical Strategies for Authentic Conversations

This section is dedicated to providing readers with actionable strategies for fostering open and honest conversations through vulnerability. We discuss active listening, empathy, and non-judgmental responses as essential tools for creating a safe space where individuals can share their vulnerabilities without fear of criticism.

Section 4: Vulnerability and Conflict Resolution

In this part, we explore how vulnerability can transform conflict resolution. By approaching conflicts with a willingness to reveal one's feelings and perspectives, individuals can de-escalate tension and build bridges to resolution. We discuss how vulnerability allows for empathy and understanding, which are crucial components of productive conflict conversations.

Section 5: Vulnerability and Self-Expression

Here, we discuss how embracing vulnerability can enhance self-expression. We explore how individuals can communicate their needs, desires, and boundaries more effectively when they are willing to be vulnerable. By sharing one's inner world, they empower themselves to communicate authentically and assertively.

Section 6: Navigating Communication Barriers

The chapter concludes by addressing common barriers to authentic communication and how vulnerability can help overcome them. We discuss issues like fear of judgment, miscommunication, and emotional avoidance. By highlighting vulnerability's role in dismantling these barriers, we empower readers to navigate even the most challenging communication scenarios.

By the end of Chapter 5, readers will understand how vulnerability is a catalyst for authentic communication. They'll be equipped with practical strategies to integrate vulnerability into their conversations, fostering connections that are built on openness, understanding, and empathy.

6

The Gift of Listening

In this chapter, we delve into the transformative power of empathetic and open listening. We explore how vulnerability and active listening go hand in hand, and we provide readers with practical techniques to engage in conversations that foster understanding and connection.

Section 1: The Essence of Empathetic Listening

We begin by highlighting the essence of empathetic listening—how it involves more than just hearing words, but also understanding the emotions, intentions, and underlying messages being conveyed. We discuss how vulnerability can only truly thrive in an environment of attentive and empathetic listening.

Section 2: Vulnerability and Active Engagement

In this part, we delve into how vulnerability encourages active engagement in conversations. By genuinely listening to someone's vulnerabilities and concerns, we show respect for their feelings and create a space where they feel heard and valued. We discuss how vulnerability and active listening contribute to mutual trust and deepening connections.

Section 3: Techniques for Effective Listening

This section is dedicated to providing readers with a toolkit of techniques for effective listening. We discuss the importance of maintaining eye contact, using open body language, and minimizing distractions to create an environment conducive to vulnerability and understanding. We also introduce the concept of reflective listening, where individuals paraphrase and summarize what they've heard to ensure accurate understanding.

Section 4: Asking Open-Ended Questions

Here, we explore the art of asking open-ended questions to encourage deeper conversations. Open-ended questions invite individuals to share more about their thoughts and feelings, promoting vulnerability and self-expression. We provide readers with examples of such questions and discuss how to use them effectively to elicit meaningful responses.

Section 5: Active Listening for Understanding Perspectives

In this part, we focus on using active listening to understand another person's perspective. We discuss how empathetic listening can help individuals see the world through the eyes of their conversation partners, fostering empathy and connection. We provide techniques for paraphrasing and validating the emotions expressed by the speaker.

Section 6: Overcoming Barriers to Listening

The chapter concludes by addressing common barriers to effective listening and how vulnerability can help overcome them. We discuss issues like preconceived judgments, emotional biases, and distractions. By emphasizing vulnerability's role in breaking down these barriers, we empower readers to become better listeners and connectors.

By the end of Chapter 6, readers will have a comprehensive understanding of how active and empathetic listening is a cornerstone of vulnerability and meaningful communication. They'll be equipped with practical techniques to engage in conversations that honor and respect the vulnerabilities shared by their partners, deepening the bonds of trust and connection.

7

Vulnerability and Emotional Intimacy

In this chapter, we explore the profound relationship between vulnerability and emotional intimacy. We delve into how opening up and sharing vulnerabilities can pave the way for deeper emotional connections and foster a level of closeness that transcends superficial interactions.

Section 1: The Role of Vulnerability in Emotional Intimacy

We begin by discussing the foundational role of vulnerability in creating emotional intimacy. Vulnerability serves as the bridge that connects two individuals at a deeper level, allowing them to share their innermost thoughts, feelings, and fears. We emphasize how vulnerability is the cornerstone upon which emotional intimacy is built.

Section 2: Creating a Safe Space for Vulnerability

Here, we delve into the importance of creating a safe and nurturing environment that encourages vulnerability. We discuss how trust, respect, and empathy are essential components of this space. By providing examples of how individuals can foster such an environment, we guide readers in becoming partners who promote vulnerability and emotional connection.

Section 3: Vulnerability's Impact on Emotional Bonds

In this part, we explore how vulnerability actively contributes to strengthening emotional bonds. We discuss how the act of sharing vulnerabilities creates a sense of mutual understanding and empathy, fostering a deeper connection between individuals. We provide real-life examples of how vulnerability has led to enduring emotional bonds in various relationship dynamics.

Section 4: Vulnerability as a Catalyst for Mutual Growth

Here, we discuss how vulnerability not only deepens emotional connections but also promotes mutual growth. By opening up about their fears, insecurities, and aspirations, individuals encourage one another to evolve and develop. We emphasize the reciprocal nature of vulnerability in fostering personal and relational growth.

Section 5: Vulnerability and Vulnerability

In this part, we delve into the concept of shared vulnerability. We discuss how when both parties are willing to open up and expose their vulnerabilities, a unique and powerful emotional connection is formed. We explore how shared vulnerability strengthens the bond between individuals by creating a sense of equality and reciprocity.

Section 6: Navigating Challenges in Pursuit of Emotional Intimacy

The chapter concludes by addressing common challenges that can arise when pursuing emotional intimacy through vulnerability. We discuss issues such as fear of rejection, navigating differing comfort levels, and the importance of setting healthy boundaries. By providing guidance on how to navigate these challenges, we empower readers to embrace vulnerability as a path to deep emotional connections.

By the end of Chapter 7, readers will have gained a comprehensive understanding of how vulnerability plays a pivotal role in creating emotional intimacy. They'll be equipped with insights and strategies to cultivate an environment that fosters vulnerability and nurtures emotional connections in a way that is meaningful, authentic, and enduring.

8

Embracing Imperfections Together

In this chapter, we delve into the importance of partners sharing vulnerabilities and imperfections within a relationship. We explore the benefits of acceptance and mutual support in cultivating a bond that transcends flaws and fosters a deeper sense of connection.

Section 1: The Strength of Vulnerability in Imperfection

We begin by discussing how embracing vulnerabilities and imperfections can actually strengthen a relationship. By acknowledging and sharing our shortcomings, we create an environment of authenticity and openness. We emphasize that being vulnerable about our imperfections allows partners to feel seen and accepted, paving the way for a more profound connection.

Section 2: The Power of Acceptance

Here, we explore the concept of acceptance as a cornerstone of a healthy and fulfilling relationship. We discuss how accepting each other's vulnerabilities and imperfections cultivates a sense of safety and emotional security. By providing examples of partners who have embraced each other's flaws, we demonstrate how acceptance leads to a more harmonious and resilient bond.

Section 3: Mutual Support and Growth

In this part, we delve into how mutual support in embracing imperfections can lead to personal and relational growth. We discuss how partners can be each other's allies in overcoming challenges and insecurities. By sharing stories of couples who have grown together through their vulnerabilities, we highlight the transformative power of mutual support.

Section 4: Vulnerability as a Bridge to Deeper Connection

Here, we discuss how vulnerability serves as a bridge to deeper emotional connections when partners are willing to reveal their imperfections. We explore how sharing vulnerabilities fosters empathy, understanding, and a genuine desire to support each other's personal growth journeys.

Section 5: The Benefits of Humility

In this part, we delve into the role of humility in embracing imperfections. We discuss how humility allows partners to recognize and admit their own limitations, fostering an environment where they can learn and grow together. We emphasize that humility paves the way for open conversations about vulnerabilities without fear of judgment.

Section 6: Navigating Challenges in Sharing Imperfections

The chapter concludes by addressing common challenges that couples may face when sharing vulnerabilities and imperfections. We discuss issues such as fear of rejection, communication barriers, and the importance of fostering a non-judgmental atmosphere. By offering guidance on navigating these challenges, we empower readers to create a relationship where sharing imperfections is not only accepted but celebrated.

By the end of Chapter 8, readers will have a comprehensive understanding of how embracing vulnerabilities and imperfections leads to deeper emotional connections. They'll be equipped with insights and strategies to create a relationship characterized by acceptance, mutual support, and a willingness to grow together despite their flaws.

9

Conflict and Vulnerability

In this chapter, we delve into the transformative potential of vulnerability in the context of conflicts within relationships. We explore how vulnerability can shift conflicts from being destructive to opportunities for growth and understanding. We also provide readers with practical strategies to address disagreements with vulnerability and empathy.

Section 1: Rethinking Conflict Through Vulnerability

We begin by challenging the conventional view of conflicts as negative experiences. We discuss how vulnerability can transform conflicts into valuable moments for emotional growth and relationship strengthening. By embracing vulnerability during conflicts, individuals open doors to deeper understanding and connection.

Section 2: The Role of Vulnerability in Conflict Resolution

In this part, we explore how vulnerability can facilitate conflict resolution.

We discuss how admitting one's mistakes, acknowledging one's emotions, and expressing one's concerns openly can create an environment where conflicts are addressed with empathy and understanding. We emphasize the power of vulnerability in promoting constructive dialogue.

Section 3: Strategies for Addressing Conflicts with Vulnerability

This section is dedicated to providing readers with practical strategies for addressing conflicts using vulnerability and empathy. We discuss techniques such as "I" statements, active listening, and perspective-taking. By showing readers how vulnerability can be applied in real conflict scenarios, we empower them to navigate disagreements with authenticity and emotional intelligence.

Section 4: Embracing Vulnerability During Heated Moments

Here, we discuss the challenges of being vulnerable during emotionally charged conflicts. We provide guidance on managing heightened emotions and staying open to vulnerability even when tensions run high. We emphasize the importance of maintaining a respectful and non-judgmental stance.

Section 5: Vulnerability as a Bridge to Understanding

In this part, we delve into how vulnerability serves as a bridge to understanding one another's perspectives during conflicts. By sharing feelings, fears, and concerns, individuals create an atmosphere where both parties can see beyond the surface of the disagreement and explore the underlying emotions driving the conflict.

Section 6: Cultivating Resilience Through Vulnerability

The chapter concludes by discussing how vulnerability not only resolves conflicts but also contributes to the resilience of a relationship. We explore how facing conflicts with vulnerability fosters trust, enhances communication, and ultimately strengthens the bond between partners.

By the end of Chapter 9, readers will have gained a comprehensive understanding of how vulnerability can transform conflicts into opportunities for growth and connection. They'll be equipped with practical strategies to address disagreements with empathy and vulnerability, promoting a deeper understanding of each other's perspectives and fostering a more resilient relationship.

10

Strengthening Bonds Through Shared Vulnerability

In this chapter, we explore the profound impact of shared vulnerability on strengthening the bonds between individuals in relationships. We discuss the benefits of opening up and sharing personal experiences, and we encourage partners to connect on a deeper level through the power of shared vulnerability.

Section 1: The Art of Sharing Personal Experiences

We begin by discussing the art of sharing personal experiences and stories. We emphasize that vulnerability goes beyond revealing emotions; it also involves opening up about past experiences, challenges, and triumphs. By sharing personal stories, individuals invite their partners into their world, creating a deeper sense of connection.

Section 2: The Benefits of Sharing Vulnerable Stories

In this part, we delve into the benefits of sharing vulnerable stories. We discuss how sharing personal experiences fosters empathy, mutual understanding, and a sense of camaraderie. By allowing partners to witness their vulnerabilities, individuals create a bond built on trust and the shared journey of growth.

Section 3: Creating a Safe Space for Sharing

Here, we explore the importance of creating a safe and judgment-free environment for sharing vulnerable stories. We discuss how partners can foster an atmosphere where both parties feel comfortable opening up about their experiences. By providing examples of empathetic responses, we guide readers in becoming supportive and receptive listeners.

Section 4: Deepening Connection Through Shared Vulnerability

In this part, we discuss how shared vulnerability leads to a deeper level of connection. By allowing partners to see different facets of each other's lives, vulnerabilities, and histories, individuals create a bond that transcends the surface. We emphasize that shared vulnerability is a way of saying, "I trust you with my past, present, and future."

Section 5: Overcoming Fear of Judgment

Here, we address the fear of judgment that often accompanies sharing vulnerable stories. We discuss strategies for overcoming this fear and embracing the idea that sharing vulnerabilities actually strengthens relationships. By encouraging self-compassion and self-acceptance, we empower individuals to share without reservation.

Section 6: Nurturing Connection Through Shared Vulnerability

The chapter concludes by offering guidance on how to continue nurturing a connection through shared vulnerability. We discuss the importance of reciprocity, active listening, and ongoing support. By highlighting the long-term benefits of consistently sharing vulnerabilities, we inspire readers to weave this practice into the fabric of their relationships.

By the end of Chapter 10, readers will have gained a comprehensive understanding of how shared vulnerability can strengthen the bonds between partners. They'll be equipped with insights and strategies to open up and share personal experiences, fostering a connection that is rooted in authenticity, empathy, and a shared journey of growth.

11

Healing and Forgiveness

In this chapter, we delve into the transformative role of vulnerability in the processes of healing and forgiveness within relationships. We explore how vulnerability can serve as a catalyst for resolution, renewal, and ultimately, the restoration of emotional well-being.

Section 1: The Power of Vulnerability in Healing

We begin by discussing how vulnerability plays a crucial role in the healing process. We explore how sharing one's pain, regrets, and wounds can lead to emotional release and catharsis. By allowing oneself to be vulnerable, individuals create a space for processing their emotions and finding solace in the support of their partner.

Section 2: Vulnerability as a Bridge to Forgiveness

In this part, we explore how vulnerability can pave the way for forgiveness. We discuss how sharing one's hurts and grievances can lead to empathy and understanding from the other party. By understanding the pain they've caused, individuals become more motivated to seek forgiveness and make amends.

Section 3: The Healing Power of Sharing Stories

Here, we delve into how sharing personal stories of pain, regret, and mistakes can promote healing and forgiveness. We provide examples of individuals who have opened up about their experiences, leading to a deeper understanding between partners and a pathway to resolution.

Section 4: Opening Up for Resolution

In this part, we discuss how opening up about one's vulnerabilities can lead to resolution of conflicts and misunderstandings. By being willing to share emotions and perspectives, individuals create an environment where problems can be addressed more effectively. We discuss how this practice promotes a sense of partnership and shared responsibility.

Section 5: Renewal Through Vulnerability

Here, we explore how vulnerability can lead to renewal and the rejuvenation of a relationship. By confronting past hurts and addressing lingering issues, individuals can create a fresh start based on understanding and mutual growth. We share stories of couples who have overcome challenges through vulnerability, emerging with stronger and more resilient bonds.

Section 6: Navigating the Path to Healing and Forgiveness

The chapter concludes by offering guidance on navigating the path to healing and forgiveness through vulnerability. We discuss the importance of patience, active listening, and empathy. By emphasizing that the journey might be challenging but ultimately rewarding, we encourage readers to embrace vulnerability as a way to heal and mend their relationships.

By the end of Chapter 11, readers will have gained a comprehensive understanding of how vulnerability can lead to healing and forgiveness within relationships. They'll be equipped with insights and examples to open up, share their pain, and navigate the path towards resolution and renewal, fostering a deeper sense of connection and emotional well-being.

12

Sustaining a Vulnerable Connection

In this final chapter, we reflect on the journey of embracing vulnerability within relationships. We summarize the key takeaways from the book and offer guidance for readers to maintain and nurture vulnerability in their connections over time.

Section 1: Reflecting on the Vulnerability Journey

We begin by reflecting on the transformative journey readers have undertaken in embracing vulnerability. We discuss how they've learned to view vulnerability as a source of strength, authenticity, and connection. We highlight the growth they've experienced in their relationships and personal lives as a result of embracing vulnerability.

Section 2: Key Takeaways and Lessons

In this part, we summarize the key takeaways and lessons from the book. We revisit the significance of vulnerability in building trust, deepening emotional intimacy, and fostering authentic connections. We emphasize the importance of empathy, active listening, and creating safe spaces for sharing vulnerabilities.

Section 3: Navigating Challenges and Celebrating Successes

Here, we discuss the challenges readers might have encountered on their journey of embracing vulnerability. We address setbacks, moments of doubt, and the fear of judgment that may have arisen. We also celebrate their successes, highlighting moments where vulnerability led to profound growth and transformation.

Section 4: The Long-Term Commitment to Vulnerability

In this part, we delve into the idea of maintaining vulnerability over the long term. We discuss how relationships evolve and change, and how sustaining vulnerability requires ongoing effort and commitment. We emphasize that vulnerability is not a one-time action but a continuous practice that enriches relationships over time.

Section 5: Cultivating Authentic Connections

Here, we offer guidance on how readers can continue cultivating authentic connections through vulnerability. We discuss the importance of checking in with each other, expressing appreciation, and creating rituals that foster vulnerability. By providing practical tips for nurturing vulnerability, we empower readers to continue reaping its benefits.

Section 6: Embracing Vulnerability in All Aspects of Life

The chapter concludes by highlighting that the lessons learned about vulnerability extend beyond relationships. We discuss how readers can apply the principles of vulnerability to other areas of life, such as friendships, family interactions, and professional collaborations. By showing that vulnerability is a life-enriching mindset, we encourage readers to fully embrace it in all aspects of their lives.

By the end of Chapter 12, readers will have reflected on their vulnerability journey and gained a comprehensive understanding of how to sustain vulnerability in their relationships. They'll be equipped with insights, guidance, and practical strategies to continue nurturing authentic connections, ultimately leading to a more fulfilling and enriched life through the power of vulnerability.

Conclusion: Embracing Vulnerability for Meaningful Connections

In closing, we reflect upon the transformative journey we've embarked upon, exploring the profound impact of vulnerability on relationships. Throughout this book, we've uncovered the intricate layers of vulnerability—the fears it entails, the trust it builds, and the authentic connections it fosters. We've witnessed how vulnerability has the power to bridge gaps, heal wounds, and create bonds that transcend the ordinary.

The lessons learned on this journey echo with one resounding truth: vulnerability is not a sign of weakness, but an emblem of strength. It's the path towards genuine connections that are rooted in authenticity, empathy, and mutual understanding. It's the practice of sharing our innermost thoughts, fears, and dreams with the courage to be seen for who we truly are.

As we close this chapter, we encourage you, the reader, to apply the invaluable lessons you've gained. Embrace vulnerability as a lifelong practice that enriches not only your relationships but your entire life. Remember that the seeds of trust are sown through your willingness to be open, honest, and compassionate. Use vulnerability as a tool to mend conflicts, deepen bonds, and ignite the flame of growth and renewal.

Let the stories, strategies, and insights shared within these pages guide you in forging connections that matter. Remember that every time you choose vulnerability, you contribute to a world where authenticity reigns, empathy flourishes, and bonds are unbreakable.

As you journey forward, may you find the strength to embrace vulnerability in its myriad forms. May you discover the joy of connecting on a level that transcends words, where hearts meet in a dance of shared experiences and mutual respect. May you become an agent of change, weaving vulnerability into the fabric of your relationships and leaving a legacy of authentic connections in your wake.

Thank you for joining us on this exploration of vulnerability's profound impact. May your path be illuminated by the power of vulnerability, leading you to connections that are genuine, enduring, and truly meaningful.

www.ingramcontent.com/pod-product-compliance
Lightning Source LLC
LaVergne TN
LVHW020457080526
838202LV00057B/6003